Fight your fears

Fighting against self-doubt and worry, facing fears with unwavering courage and commitment. Make fear a catalyst for your strength, resilience, and personal progress by embracing discomfort.

By

January Smith

Table of Contents

Chapter 1

Understanding Fear 1

   1.1   Defining Fear: A Complex Emotion 5

   1.2   Types of Fear: Rational vs. Irrational....................................7

   1.3   The Role of Fear in Human Evolution................................... 11

Chapter 2

The Psychology of Fear......................... 14

   2.1 How Fear is Processed in the Brain 17

   2.2 The Fight-or-Flight Response: Unraveling Fear's Effects................... 20

   2.3 Conditioning and Fear: Breaking the Cycle...................................23

Chapter 3

Identifying Your Fears.........................27

   3.1 Unveiling Hidden Fears: Self-Reflection and Awareness................... 31

   3.2 Common Fears: Exploring Fear's Universality.................................34

3.3 Root Causes of Fear: Digging Deeper....................36

Chapter 4

Confronting Fear: Strategies and Techniques............................ 40

4.1 Gradual Exposure: Step-by-Step Approach....................................45

4.2 Cognitive Restructuring: Changing Fearful Thinking Patterns.................. 49

4.3 Meditation and Mindfulness: Cultivating Inner Strength..................54

Chapter 5

Overcoming Fear of Failure.................. 58

5.1 Understanding the Fear of Failure: Its Impact on Success 62

5.2 Embracing Failure: A Catalyst for Growth and Learning..........................65

5.3 Building Resilience: Bouncing Back from Setbacks 68

Chapter 6

Navigating Social Anxiety.....................72

6.1 Social Anxiety: The Fear of Judgment and Rejection.....................75

6.2 Building Social Confidence: Tips and Techniques 79

6.3 Expanding Social Networks: Overcoming Isolation 83

Chapter 7

Overcoming Fear of Change 86

7.1 Fear of the Unknown: Embracing Life Transitions 88

7.2 Embracing Change: Strategies for Adaptability 89

7.3 Thriving in Uncertainty: Seizing Change's Opportunities 91

Chapter 8

Managing Fear in Relationships 93

8.1 Fear of Intimacy: Overcoming Emotional Barriers 94

8.2 Communication and Vulnerability: Building Trust 95

8.3 Healing Past Wounds: Letting Go of Fear in Relationships 97

Chapter 9

Cultivating Courage and Self-Confidence 100

9.1 Developing Inner Strength: The Power of Courage 102

9.2 Techniques and Practices for Increasing Self-Confidence 105

9.3 Taking Action: Stepping Outside the Comfort Zone 106

Chapter 10

Sustaining Progress and Embracing a Fearless Life 109

10.1 Maintaining Fearlessness: Strategies for Long-Term Success 111

10.2 Embracing Growth: Continuing the Journey Beyond Fears 112

10.3 Inspiring Others: Spreading Courage and Empowerment 114

Fight Your Fears

Chapter 1

Understanding Fear

Fear is an inherent part of the human experience. It is a strong and complex feeling that has the potential to significantly affect our lives. Although fear is frequently considered a negative emotion, it actually plays a crucial role in our survival and can reveal significant information about who we really are. We can learn to handle fear more effectively and take advantage of its potential for development and transformation by understanding it and its root causes.

Fear can appear in a variety of ways, from quiet unease to utter fear. It may result from internal thoughts and beliefs or be brought on by outside conditions. Fear is basically a reaction to perceived threats, whether they are actual or imagined. Our fight-or-flight reaction is triggered, ready us to either face the danger head-on or flee from it.

The fear of the unknown is among the most prevalent phobias. It results from our innate desire for stability and predictability. When faced with uncertainty, we tend to imagine the worst-case situations, which breeds worry and fear. Accepting uncertainty, however, can serve as an avenue for development and self-discovery. We may broaden our perspectives and improve our resilience in the face of uncertainty by moving outside of our comfort zones.

The fear of failing is another common phobia. A lot of us have been taught to associate failure with inadequacy and shame. Failure, however, is an essential component of learning and a prerequisite for success. We may overcome our anxiety and pursue our goals with greater confidence and tenacity if we reframe our perspective on failure and see it as a chance for growth and self-improvement.

Fear may also have roots in traumatic events and the past. These encounters leave lasting marks on our brain and have the power to influence our ideas and actions. Recognizing and processing our feelings, asking for help from friends and family or professionals, and building resilience are all necessary for recovering from prior traumas. We can break free from the hold of our previous fears and live more completely in the present by confronting them.

dread of abandonment or rejection is another component of fear. We desire belonging and recognition because we are social beings. The fear of being rejected or abandoned can hinder our ability to form meaningful connections and lead to isolation. Building self-worth and self-acceptance, fostering good connections, and accepting vulnerability are necessary to get over this anxiety. By letting go of the need for constant validation, we can forge deeper connections based on authenticity and mutual respect. By letting go of the need for constant validation, we can forge deeper connections based on authenticity and mutual respect.

We can use fear as a compass to direct us toward our most fervent aspirations and passions. The things we fear the most may occasionally be the things that hold the key to our own personal development and fulfillment. We can find hidden strengths and realize our full potential by facing our anxieties and accepting discomfort.

We must also acknowledge that fear is a subjective experience that varies considerably from person to person if we are to comprehend it. One person's experience of terror may not be the same as another person. It's crucial to handle fear with compassion and empathy, both for oneself and for others. We may establish a safe space that encourages development and understanding if we acknowledge and appreciate one another's worries.

1.1 Defining Fear: A Complex Emotion

Fear is a complex and innate human emotion that has played a crucial role in our evolutionary development. By warning us of potential dangers and risks in our environment, it functions as a key survival tactics. Although fear is frequently considered to be a bad feeling, it actually plays a vital part in our lives by encouraging us to take the necessary measures and make wise decisions. Understanding the origins, causes, and manifestations of fear might help us gain important insights into how people think and feel.

An emotional reaction to a perceived threat or danger is known as fear. It is characterized by a strong sense of dread that is accompanied by physiological responses such a faster heartbeat, shallow breathing, and heightened senses. This reaction has its roots in our evolutionary past and stems from our innate desire to defend oneself from danger.

The things that cause dread might differ greatly from person to person. Some popular phobias, like the dread of spiders, darkness, or heights, have their roots in our primitive instincts. These fears can be influenced by cultural or personal causes and are frequently acquired early in life. Other fears are more complicated and can be influenced by our unique beliefs, experiences, and societal upbringing. Examples include the fear of failure, rejection, or the unknown.

Different types of fear might appear, from slight uneasiness to paralyzing panic. It may cause us to have a fight-or-flight reaction, causing us to either confront the feared threat or run for cover. The excessive and unreasonable forms of fear, on the other hand, can result in phobias and anxiety disorders that have significant adverse effects on a person's day-to-day activities.

For many people, getting past fear is a huge hurdle. It requires figuring out the main causes and creating efficient defenses. Some of the methods used to help people manage and overcome their phobias include relaxation techniques, cognitive-behavioral therapy, and exposure therapy. Not all concerns must be overcome; rather, a healthy balance must be struck that enables people to live fulfilling lives while remaining conscious of the risks they may face.

Fear affects society structures and collective behavior in addition to personal experiences. Governments, institutions, and the media can use it as a tool of control to sway people's opinions and actions. For a society to remain healthy and balanced and free from violence, bigotry, and prejudice, it is essential to understand how fear functions on a societal level.

Although fear can be a strong and overwhelming feeling, it can also be a source of development and self-discovery. Taking on our fears can help us grow as people, become more resilient, and have more self-confidence. It forces us to step outside of our comfort zones, allowing us to consider novel alternatives and broaden our perspectives.

1.2 Types of Fear: Rational vs. Irrational

Fear is a normal human emotion that has both positive and negative effects. It acts as a safeguard by warning us of possible dangers and urging caution. But fear can also become illogical, leading to unneeded anxiety and impeding personal development. In order to manage and overcome fear, one must be able to distinguish between reasonable and irrational fear. We shall examine these two forms of fear's properties and effects on daily life in this post.

Real and useful, rational fear is also referred to as healthy fear. It is an answer to actual threats or impending peril. For instance, it seems sense to be scared when you run into a wild animal or are in fear of losing your life. This kind of fear sets off our body's natural defenses, allowing us to respond appropriately. It also sets off our fight-or-flight reaction. Because it aids us in avoiding injury and making wise judgments in dangerous situations, rational fear is adaptive.

On the other side, excessive and disproportionate to the actual threat is irrational fear, often known as phobia or anxiety. It frequently results from fictitious or unreasonable events. Even when there is no genuine danger around, people with irrational fears may experience severe anxiety or panic attacks when exposed to their fear-inducing stimuli. Irrational fears frequently manifest as a fear of flying, a fear of spiders, or a fear of public speaking. These anxieties can have a considerable negative effect on a person's daily life, restricting their experiences and resulting in needless suffering.

The degree of threat present is one important distinction between rational and irrational anxiety. Irrational worries are caused by imagined threats that are frequently unjustified, whereas rational fears are based on real worries. Irrational fears require a more involved strategy to treat the underlying anxiety or phobia, but rational concerns can be addressed by taking precautions and making sense-based decisions.

Furthermore, once the threat has passed, reasonable fear usually dissipates quickly. It has no negative effects on a person's capacity to carry out daily tasks. On the other hand, illogical fear can linger for a long time and result in persistent uneasiness and discomfort. It might result in avoidance behaviors, when people go to great lengths to avoid things that make them feel afraid. This would only serve to highlight how irrational the fear response is.

Therapy, exposure techniques, and cognitive-behavioral methods are frequently used in conjunction to treat irrational fear. Individuals can learn coping mechanisms to deal with anxiety and the underlying causes of their fears with the aid of therapy. By gradually exposing oneself to the feared stimuli in a safe atmosphere, exposure approaches help people face their fears and understand that the impending danger is either overstated or nonexistent. By questioning erroneous thought patterns and substituting them with more sensible viewpoints, cognitive-behavioral therapy assists people in reshaping their thoughts and beliefs regarding their fear.

1.3 The Role of Fear in Human Evolution

An intricate and powerful emotion, fear has played significantly to the development of the human species. Throughout the course of our evolutionary history, it has been a crucial survival strategy that has allowed us to identify and respond to possible threats. Fear has influenced our behavior, cognition, and even our physical characteristics from the dawn of humanity to the present, eventually influencing our survival and prosperity as a species.

Promoting self-preservation is one of fear's main purposes. Fear sets off a series of physiological reactions, including a faster heartbeat, sharpened senses, and the production of stress hormones like adrenaline, when there is danger. These reactions set the body up for a fight-or-flight reaction, enabling people to either face the threat or run away from it. When facing predators or other life-threatening events, our ancestors' instinctual response to fear has been essential.

In addition, fear has been crucial to the evolution of the human brain. Processing fear and triggering the fear response are the responsibilities of the amygdala, a deep brain area. The human brain has changed over time to become extremely alert to possible threats, enabling quick and adaptable reactions. Because of their improved ability to recognize and avoid danger, this heightened fear response has given humans a survival advantage and allowed them to pass on their genetic heritage.

The development of communities and human social behavior have both been impacted by fear. People had to work together to overcome several obstacles in early human history in order to survive. Humans formed groups out of a sense of security and to protect themselves from outside threats. This increased their chances of surviving. Fear-based social bonding encouraged resource sharing, work division, and the development of complex social structures, all of which aided in the success of our evolutionary efforts.

Additionally, fear has significantly influenced the development of the human race. Fear has always been the motivation behind rituals, religious beliefs, and cultural behaviors. The founding of religious institutions and the development of mythology were prompted by a fear of the unknown and a desire to find protection from supernatural powers. These cultural institutions gave people a sense of security, answers to existential queries, and a conceptual framework for comprehending and navigating life's uncertainties.

While fear has played a crucial role in our evolutionary development, it can also have unfavorable effects. An individual's everyday functioning and quality of life can be negatively impacted by anxiety disorders and phobias, which are caused by excessive or illogical anxieties. As seen by examples of propaganda and fear-based manipulation in all facets of society, fear can also be used and exploited.

Chapter 2
The Psychology of Fear

Fear is a powerful, complex emotion that has a strong psychological basis. It is a natural defense system that is part of our instinctive response to potential threats and danger. Knowing the psychology of fear can help us better understand how it affects our ideas, actions, and general wellbeing.

The power of dread to cause our bodies to go into a stress response is one of the main features of fear. The amygdala, a region of the brain in charge of processing emotions, particularly fear, receives messages from our brains when we sense a threat. A series of physiological changes, including faster heart rate, shallower breathing, and enhanced attention, are then triggered by the amygdala. We are prepared for fight, flight, or freeze reactions thanks to these reactions.

Furthermore, the idea of conditioning is closely related to the emotion of fear. Our brains learn to associate particular stimuli with fear responses through experiences and associations. It's possible for this programming to be both helpful and harmful. For instance, even if not all dogs are dangerous, someone who has a traumatic experience with a dog may grow afraid of all dogs. It can be difficult to get over this entrenched fear, and it could result in anxiety disorders.

The psychology of fear is significantly influenced by cognitive factors as well. The strength and duration of our fear responses can be significantly influenced by our beliefs and how we interpret things. For instance, catastrophic thinking might increase fear since it includes seeing the worst-case possibilities. On the other hand, fear can be managed and reduced with the aid of cognitive restructuring techniques, such as confronting irrational thoughts and replacing them with rational ones.

Fear can also be impacted by society. Humans are social beings, and our behavior can be greatly influenced by our fear of social rejection or criticism. The fear over being negatively judged frequently forces people to conform and prevents them from being themselves. It can lead to social anxiety and a constant need for validation.

For personal development and wellbeing, it is crucial to comprehend the psychology of fear. People can create plans to control and get rid of their worries by becoming aware of the causes and underlying mechanisms of fear. People have found success using strategies like exposure therapy, mindfulness, and cognitive-behavioral therapy to confront and manage their fear responses.

2.1 How Fear is Processed in the Brain

Fear is a natural and instinctual feeling that is essential to our survival. It assists us in defending against potential dangers and adjusting to our surroundings. Understanding the complex mechanisms underlying fear requires an understanding of how the brain interprets this emotion. This article will address the neural structures involved in processing fear and give light on the intricate interactions that take place between various brain areas during fear responses.

The Amygdala and Fear Conditioning:

The amygdala, a brain region with an almond shape, is at the center of how fear is interpreted. The amygdala is primarily responsible for detecting and processing fear-related stimuli. It gathers sensory information from the surroundings and quickly assesses the emotional meaning of the information. The amygdala creates a learned fear response by associating a neutral stimulus with a bad experience, a process known as fear conditioning. Our capacity to anticipate threats and react to them depends on this process.

Neural Pathways Involved in Fear: The thalamus and the cortex are the two main pathways via which sensory data is transmitted to the amygdala when we face a threatening stimuli, such as a dangerous animal or a loud noise. The thalamic pathway offers a quick and direct route that enables quick responses to danger that is approaching. The cerebral pathway, in contrast, processes more specific information about the stimulus, enabling a more complex evaluation of the threat.

The Prefrontal Cortex's Function:

Processing of fear is mostly governed by the prefrontal cortex (PFC), a region engaged in higher-order cognitive functions. It acts as a top-down control mechanism, regulating and modulating the amygdala's response to frightening stimuli. The PFC aids in explaining the fear-inspiring stimuli, assessing their importance, and controlling fear reactions appropriately. This circuitry's dysfunction can affect adaptive fear responses and be a factor in anxiety disorders.

Neurotransmitters and Fear:

The processing of fear is significantly influenced by neurotransmitters, which are chemical messengers in the brain. Glutamate and gamma-aminobutyric acid (GABA) are two important neurotransmitters that are involved. While GABA functions as an inhibitory neurotransmitter, suppressing impulses associated with fear, glutamate increases the amygdala's excitability, increasing fear reactions. Disorders associated with fear, such as post-traumatic stress disorder (PTSD), may be influenced by imbalances in these neurotransmitter systems.

The amygdala triggers the hypothalamic-pituitary-adrenal (HPA) axis, a critical stress response mechanism, in response to a stimuli that causes fear. The hypothalamus, pituitary, and adrenal glands are all part of this axis. Corticotropin-releasing hormone (CRH), which is released by the brain, causes the pituitary gland to release adrenocorticotropic hormone (ACTH). Cortisol is one of the stress hormones that are released by the adrenal glands as a result of ACTH. These hormones improve our capacity to respond to the perceived threat by preparing the body for a fight-or-flight reaction.

Modulating Fear Responses:

In order to develop new treatments for illnesses linked to fear, researchers have made enormous progress in understanding how fear is processed. Techniques like exposure therapy and cognitive-behavioral therapy (CBT) try to rewire the fear response by exposing people to feared stimuli gradually in a controlled setting. By modifying neurotransmitter levels, pharmacological treatments like selective serotonin reuptake inhibitors (SSRIs) can also be successful in treating anxiety disorders.

2.2 The Fight-or-Flight Response: Unraveling Fear's Effects

The basic feeling of fear has evolved to aid both humans and other animals in reacting to perceived threats. The fight-or-flight reaction is a complex physiological response that the body initiates when faced with a frightening scenario. This response starts a chain reaction that prepares the body to either face the threat head-on or flee from it. Scientists have gotten a better understanding of this unique survival strategy by analyzing how fear affects the body.

The sympathetic nervous system, which controls the body's natural reflexes, is what drives the fight-or-flight response. The amygdala in the brain plays a critical role in perceiving the threat and starting the response when fear is detected. It activates numerous bodily systems by sending distress signals to the hypothalamus, which serves as a command center.

The adrenal glands release stress chemicals, notably adrenaline and cortisol, as the first observable result of the fight-or-flight response. The bloodstream is suddenly flooded with adrenaline, which immediately raises heart rate and blood pressure. This increased cardiovascular response assists in preparing the body for physical exercise by supplying nutrients and oxygen to the muscles.

The release of glucose for an energy surge is facilitated concurrently by an increase in cortisol levels. The body's ability to react quickly to threat depends on this energy mobilization. Blood supply to non-essential organs, such as the digestive and reproductive systems, decreases as blood flow to the muscles increases, temporarily limiting their functioning.

Additionally, the fight-or-flight response triggers changes in the respiratory system. In order to maximize oxygen intake and support the body's increased activity, breathing becomes quick and shallow. To improve visual perception and improve the ability to identify potential hazards, the eyes dilate. The ability to hear and feel more clearly also heightens sensitivity to potential danger.

Fear also has an impact on brain activity. During the fight-or-flight reaction, the prefrontal cortex, which is in charge of rational thought and decision-making, becomes less active. As the attention shifts to immediate survival, the ability to think clearly and critically is impaired by this decreased activity.

The fight-or-flight response is necessary for survival, but it can be harmful if it is activated too much or for too long. Chronic stress brought on by frequent exposure to anxiety or terror can result in a number of health difficulties, including immune system deterioration, heart problems, and mental health disorders.

The creation of efficient treatments has been made possible by our growing understanding of the intricacies of the fight-or-flight response. People can control their fear responses with the aid of methods like mindfulness, deep breathing exercises, and cognitive-behavioral therapy, which supports a balanced emotional and physiological state.

2.3 Conditioning and Fear: Breaking the Cycle

Fear and conditioning are interconnected elements of human behavior that frequently result in the continuation of harmful practices and limit personal development.

Fear is a reaction to perceived threats or dangers whereas conditioning is the process of learning to and adapting to certain stimuli or conditions. Individuals must end the cycle of conditioning and fear if they are to overcome obstacles and embrace their own development.

Early in childhood, we begin to establish beliefs and learn knowledge from our environment, including our family, culture, and society. These imprinted patterns serve as the foundation for our conditioned responses, shaping our ideas, emotions, and behaviors. For instance, if a child grows up in a setting where criticism is common, they could have a fear of failing and learn to constantly seek approval.

On the other hand, fear is an instinctive and normal reaction to possible damage. It acts as a protect, getting us ready to react to threats. However, when fear takes on an unreasonable or exaggerated form, it can impede personal development and restrict our experiences. There are many typical fears that can prevent people from moving outside of their comfort zones, including fear of the unknown, fear of failure, and fear of judgment.

It takes intentional effort and a willingness to question deeply rooted beliefs and habits to break the cycle of conditioning and fear. Self-awareness, which entails understanding and accepting our enlightenment and the concerns that result from it, is a crucial component. We can learn more about our cognitive processes and emotional reactions by practicing mindfulness and introspection.

Breaking the cycle requires education and exposure to many viewpoints. We can extend our views and confront preconceived assumptions by pursuing information and comprehending many points of view. This gives us the ability to challenge the truth of our conditioned ideas and make decisions that are in line with our true selves.

Face-to-face communication with our concerns is another crucial element. We might gradually become less sensitive to the imagined threats that cause fear by stepping outside of our comfort zones and embracing discomfort. Building confidence and resilience through taking baby steps, establishing realistic goals, and celebrating accomplishments might help us overcome the constraints imposed by conditioning and fear.

Therapy and support networks can both be quite helpful in ending the pattern. A secure environment to explore our anxieties, address underlying traumas, and develop coping mechanisms is provided by seeking advice from dependable mentors, therapists, or support groups. These resources provide insight, inspiration, and useful tools to help people deal with the difficult process of self-transformation.

It is significant to remember that ending the cycle of conditioning and fear is an ongoing process of self-discovery and development rather than a linear one. It calls for endurance, compassion, and patience. Although each person's journey will be different and their progress may fluctuate, the key lies in their dedication to growth and their fortitude to confront deeply rooted habits.

Chapter 3

Fear is a common human emotion that has different forms and effects on different people. It is a natural reaction made to defend us from perceived threats or dangers. Although fear can be useful in certain situations, it can also prevent us from reaching our greatest potential and living fulfilling lives. Therefore, it is essential that we acknowledge and understand our fears in order to get over them and develop as people. In this post, we'll discuss how crucial it is to recognize your concerns and offer a few strategies to aid you in doing so.

The first step to improving yourself is to face your worries and acknowledge them. In the hope that they will simply go away, many people have a tendency to avoid or repress their concerns. But using this approach just makes dread more powerful in its grip. We gain a more profound understanding of ourselves and improve our ability to deal effectively with our concerns by facing them.

One way to identify your fears is through self-reflection. When you are faced with challenging situations, give your thoughts and feelings some thought. What ideas come to mind? What feelings do you have in your body? You can identify the underlying fears that may be influencing your conduct by paying attention to your internal reactions.

Journaling is a further helpful method. Make time every day to write about your worries and fears. Putting your ideas down on paper might help you become more clear-headed and more objective. Write honestly and without inhibition. This method might make you aware of fears you may not have known about or dismissed as unimportant.

Talking openly and honestly with dependable friends or family members can also be helpful. Sometimes looking at things from a different angle can reveal fears that may be deeply ingrained yet are hidden from our own vision. Encourage individuals who care about you and understand you to offer their thoughts and views by enlisting their help.

In addition to self-reflection and external input, it is important to pay attention to recurring patterns in your life. Pay attention to situations or behaviors that frequently cause fear or discomfort. These patterns may offer hints as to the underlying fears that require addressing. By recognizing these patterns, you can focus on particular areas of personal development.

It is important to note that fear frequently coexists with other emotions like insecurity, traumatic experiences, or low self-esteem. You can dispel complex fears that may have ingrained roots by understanding these connections. To assist you with this process, you can think about getting professional assistance from therapy or counseling. A qualified therapist can offer insightful advice and practical strategies to assist you in successfully overcoming your concerns.

Once you've recognized your fears, it's important to approach them gradually and under control. Start by establishing modest, achievable goals that allow you to experience your fears in a secure context. For instance, if you're afraid of public speaking, start by doing it in front of a small, encouraging group. As your confidence grows, progressively up the difficulty until you can speak in front of larger crowds without feeling uncomfortable.

Keep in mind that overcoming fear requires patience and time. Throughout the process, be fair to yourself and acknowledge all of your successes. Encouragement and affirmations that support your confidence that you can face your anxieties should be all around you.

3.1 Unveiling Hidden Fears: Self-Reflection and Awareness

We use self-reflection and awareness as vital tools on our path to personal development. We discover hidden fears that may obstruct our development and fulfillment by diving deeply into ourselves. These fears frequently show up in different areas of our lives, having an effect on our relationships, professional decisions, and general wellbeing. We can better comprehend these concerns through the process of self-reflection and then take preventative measures to deal with and get rid of them.

Introspection and analysis of our ideas, feelings, and behaviors are both components of self-reflection. It requires establishing an atmosphere of safety free from judgment and outside influences where one may honestly evaluate oneself. This procedure can be aided by practicing techniques like journaling, meditation, or going to therapy, which enables us to peel back the layers of our psyche.

We come upon repressed fears that have influenced our lives as we travel the path of self-reflection. These fears may be brought on by previous experiences, societal norms, or self-imposed restrictions. Fear of the unknown, fear of vulnerability, fear of rejection, and fear of failure are a few examples. These fears frequently serve as barriers that keep us from going after our goals, being true in our expression, or embracing new opportunities.

We start reducing these hidden fear power over us by bringing them to light. We understand that they frequently stem from unreasonable beliefs or misguided impressions. Self-awareness gives us the power to confront these fears and swap out negative thoughts for positive ones. We can release self-imposed restrictions and realize our true potential through this procedure.

Additionally, self-reflection enables us to spot trends and triggers connected to our concerns. We can discover the root causes of these fears and follow them all the way back to the beginning. We gain important understandings about ourselves and our behaviour from this deep understanding. With this understanding, we can create coping mechanisms and overcoming tactics for our concerns.

Self-reflection also promotes compassion and empathy for oneself. We understand that everyone has fears to some degree because they are a natural aspect of being human. We learn to face our fears with kindness and understanding rather of criticizing ourselves for feeling them. This kind of self-compassion fosters an environment that supports development and resilience.

Self-reflection and awareness have a significant impact on our interpersonal connections in addition to promoting personal progress. We gain a heightened sensitivity to the fears and vulnerabilities of those around us as we become more aware of our own fears. Empathy makes our connections stronger and makes it possible for us to assist and understand others on their own journeys.

3.2 Common Fears: Exploring Fear's Universality

Fear is a strong and pervasive emotion that has always played a significant role in the history of humanity. It is a natural reaction to perceived threats or risks, and people of all ages and cultures exhibit it. Even while the exact sources of fear can change, the fundamental processes and bodily reactions are fairly stable. This essay explores the universal concerns that all people have while offering light on their psychological and evolutionary relevance.

The fear of dying is one of the most basic fears that all humans experience. The fear of death is imprinted firmly in our collective psyche, whether it takes the form of a fear of one's own mortality or a fear of losing loved ones. The fear is a result of humans' innate desire to survive and preserve their genetic heritage. It transcends social and cultural barriers, bringing people from many origins together in their shared fear of the inevitable end of life.

Fear of the unknown is yet another irrational fear. Humans are creatures of habit and familiarity, seeking comfort in the familiar and predictable. The unknown, however, poses a potential risk since it breeds doubt and irrationality. This fear can be seen in many different facets of life, including exploring uncharted territory, going through novel experiences, and meeting new people. The fear of the unknown serves as a defense mechanism, alerting us to prospective threats and preparing us for them.

Human nature is also strongly ingrained with a fear of being rejected and social exclusion. Humans naturally crave approval and inclusion in their societies since they are social beings. The worry of isolation or rejection, which can endanger our social standing and psychological well-being, is the root of the fear of rejection. This fear drives people to follow social norms, look for approval, and preserve relationships, preserving the cohesion of social groups.

Another common dread that cuts across cultures and time periods is the fear of failing. It comes from a desire for recognition, success, and accomplishment.

People who are paralyzed by their fear of failing are unable to take risks or work toward their objectives. Because failure is frequently linked to feelings of inadequacy or incompetence, this fear is intimately related to self-esteem issues and the fear of being judged. For personal development, it's essential to get over the failure fear.

Last but not least, everyone has a common fear of losing something. The loss of loved ones, possessions, status, or even one's own identity are all included in this fear. Because loss is intrinsically painful and upsetting, people take measures and protect their most prized possessions out of dread of suffering such pain. Our attachments and the importance we give to the people and things in our lives are highlighted by this fear.

3.3 Root Causes of Fear: Digging Deeper

Being afraid is a natural human feeling that has been imprinted in our mind since the beginning of time. When left unchecked, fear can be a protective mechanism that serves to alert us to impending risks, but it can also impede personal development and wellbeing. We must go deeper into its underlying causes in order to fully comprehend fear and how it affects our lives. We can learn important lessons and create effective coping mechanisms by investigating the root causes of fear.

The fear of the unknown is one of the main reasons of fear. We have a natural desire for predictability and assurance as humans. The absence of knowledge and comprehension caused by the unknown can make us fearful and nervous. The uncertainty of the future can cause worry, whether it is while starting a new career or relationship. We may lessen the force of the unknown and widen our horizons by embracing uncertainty and creating a curiosity-based mindset.

Traumatic past events are another important source of fear. Accidents, failures, or abuse incidents can leave us with lasting emotional scars that affect how we perceive the world and behave in the future. These incidents trigger a fear reaction in an effort to protect us from further harm. In order to address and heal the underlying wounds, overcoming fear rooted in prior experiences can often require professional assistance, such as therapy or counseling. We may gradually loosen the hold these traumas have on our lives by acknowledging and processing them.

Additionally, social conditioning is also important in the growth of fear. We pick up society standards, cultural beliefs, and other people's expectations from an early age. These outside factors affect how we perceive what is risky and safe, frequently creating illogical worries or phobias. Questioning and critically analyzing our views, looking for a balanced viewpoint, and actively deciding which worries are grounded in reality and which are based on false assumptions are all necessary steps in challenging cultural conditioning.

Fear of failure and rejection is another fundamental source of fear. Many of our actions and choices are influenced by our desire for approval and validation. We can get frozen by our fear of failing or of being criticized by others, which keeps us from taking chances or pursuing our aspirations. It's crucial to practice self-compassion and reframe failure as a chance for personal development if you want to get over this fear. We can gradually overcome the fear of failure and pursue our goals with greater resiliency by accepting setbacks as useful lessons and learning that rejection does not determine our worth.

Last but not least, fear can be exacerbated by the media and information overload of today's environment. Negative occurrences are frequently sensationalized by news organizations, which distorts people's perceptions of reality. Continuous exposure to scary tales might intensify feelings of fear and anxiety. To manage this element of fear, media literacy exercises and limiting exposure to frightening material are recommended.

Chapter 4

Confronting Fear: Strategies and Techniques

Fear is a natural human emotion that takes many forms and frequently gets in the way of progress, achievement, and general wellbeing. However, people may face and conquer their fears, enabling them to lead more satisfying lives, by comprehending fear and implementing useful ideas and techniques. This article examines the nature of fear, its effects on people, and offers helpful methods and strategies for facing and overcoming fear.

Identifying Fear:

A primitive instinct, fear serves to keep us safe from harm. It sets off a fight-or-flight reaction, enabling the body to react swiftly to dangers. While fear can be necessary in instances where life is at risk, it frequently becomes unreasonable and overwhelming, having a detrimental effect on one's ability to advance personally and professionally.

The Effects of Fear: Fear has the power to immobilize people, preventing them from achieving their objectives and desires. It prevents one from expanding outside their comfort zone. Missed chances, self-doubt, worry, and low self-esteem can all be caused by fear. Therefore, it is imperative to create plans and methods for facing fear head-on and overcoming its crippling consequences.

Strategies for Overcoming Fear:

1. Identify and Acknowledge Fear: Recognizing and acknowledging fear is the first step in overcoming it. The fundamental reasons and triggers of fear can be discovered through self-reflection and introspection. People

can start overcoming their concerns by identifying them specifically.

2. Educate Yourself: Uncertainty and ignorance are two things that typically feed fear. Learning more about the thing you're afraid of can help you feel in control and eliminate unreasonable ideas. People who are empowered by knowledge are better able to face their worries and make wise judgments.

3. Establish Realistic Goals: You may make your goals less intimidating by breaking them down into smaller, more attainable steps. Setting attainable goals helps people feel like they are making progress, which boosts confidence and lowers fear.

4. Visualize Success: Successful people in a wide range of professions employ the potent tool of visualization. You can teach your mind to have confidence in your skills by visualizing yourself facing and conquering your fears. This encouraging feedback can reduce

anxiety and improve your chances of success.

5. Practice Exposure: Exposure to frightening circumstances or stimuli over time might help the mind become desensitized and lessen the intensity of dread. Start out slowly and raise the exposure amount progressively over time. Exposure therapy is a method that can help people overcome their phobias and anxieties.

Techniques for Overcoming Fear:

1. **Deep Breathing and Relaxation:** When we experience fear, our body frequently react by contracting our muscles and shallow breathing. Deep breathing exercises and relaxation methods like yoga or meditation can assist the body and mind relax and quiet down, lowering fear and anxiety.

2. **Positive Affirmations**: Use positive affirmations in place of negative self-talk. Affirmations are statements that support good aims and beliefs. Affirmations like "I am capable" and "I

can overcome my fears" can help people reorganize their mental processes and boost their confidence.

3. **Seek Support:** Facing fear can be difficult, and getting help from friends, family, or experts can be a helpful source of direction and inspiration. Joining support groups or going to counseling can provide a safe environment where you can share experiences, get new perspectives, and get advice on overcoming fear.

4. **Take Calculated Risks**: Leaving one's comfort zone is crucial for personal development. People can increase their abilities and build resilience by taking reasonable risks and eventually pushing over their fears. A decreased fear about making mistakes can also result from accepting failure as a teaching opportunity.

5. **Celebrate Small Victories**: Recognize and honor each step taken in overcoming fear. By celebrating little achievements, people can build on their success and increase their

self-confidence, which encourages positive thinking and spurs on further development.

4.1 Gradual Exposure: Step-by-Step Approach

In the field of psychology, gradual exposure, usually referred to as systematic desensitization, is a common therapeutic method for the treatment of anxiety disorders. It involves a step-by-step process that gradually exposes people to the feared stimuli or situations in order to assist them overcome their fears and anxieties. This approach has shown to be quite successful in assisting individuals in creating coping mechanisms and ultimately lowering their anxiety levels. The ideas of gradual exposure will be thoroughly covered in this essay, along with its step-by-step methodology.

Understanding Gradual Exposure

According to the theory of classical conditioning, which is the foundation for gradual exposure, fears and anxieties can be unlearned by associating what is feared with relaxation and rewarding events. The procedure is building a hierarchy of frightening scenarios, going from the least unsettling to the most upsetting. People can gradually increase their tolerance for these events and lessen their anxiety responses by being exposed to them repeatedly in a safe and supportive atmosphere.

Step-by-Step Procedure

1. **Identifying the Fear**: Identification of the specific fear or anxiety that has to be addressed is the first step in progressive exposure. This could be any phobia, such as a fear of heights, public speaking, or social situations. For the exposure exercises to be successful, a thorough knowledge of the fear is essential.

2. **Establishing a Fear Hierarchy**: The next stage is to establish a hierarchy of fears once the fear has been identified. This is dissecting the dread into a succession of more manageable tasks or situations and organizing them in ascending anxiety. If you're afraid of flying, for instance, the hierarchy might include looking at

photographs of airplanes, going to an airport, getting on a plane, and then experiencing a little flight.

3. **Progressive Muscle Relaxation**: It's important to educate people relaxation techniques like progressive muscle relaxation before they start the exposure activities. During the exposure phase, this teaches children how to relax their muscles and control their anxiety.

4. **Exposure to the Least Anxious Step:** The person is gradually exposed to the circumstance that causes the least amount of anxiety, starting with the first step in the fear hierarchy. While executing relaxation exercises, they are urged to imagine or feel the situation in question. The exposure should continue up to a considerable reduction in their fear.

5. **Gradually Increasing Exposure**: Once the person is at ease with the first stage in the hierarchy, they can move on to the following one. Each step should be a little more difficult than the one before it, building on the

advancement made. The level of comfort and readiness of the individual should dictate the rate of growth.

6. **Reinforcement and Positive Associations**: It's critical to offer encouragement and supportive feedback at every stage of the exposure process. This increases people's confidence in their ability to effectively manage their anxiety and helps them form positive associations with the fearful events.

7. **Generalization and Maintenance**: People learn to generalize their newly acquired skills to real-life circumstances as they go up the hierarchy and effectively face their concerns. The coping mechanisms they learnt during the exposure process can subsequently be used to maintain their improvement.

4.2 Cognitive Restructuring: Changing Fearful Thinking Patterns

A potent psychological method called cognitive restructuring tries to alter unfavorable and fearful thought patterns. It is predicated on the idea that our thoughts have a significant impact on our feelings and actions. Cognitive restructuring assists people in replacing illogical beliefs with more adaptive and rational ones by recognizing and addressing them. Anxiety, dread, and other negative emotions may be lessened as a result of this process. This essay will examine the basic principles of cognitive restructuring and go over useful tactics for altering anxious thought patterns.

Understanding Fearful Thinking Patterns:

Cognitive distortions, which are biased and unreasonable ways of viewing reality, are frequently present in the thought processes associated with fear. Fear and anxiety can be amplified by these distortions. Typical cognitive distortions include the following:

1. **Catastrophizing:** Exaggerating how serious a situation is and assuming the worst.
2. **Overgeneralization:** Making assumptions based on a single negative experience or event.
3. **Personalization:** Assuming responsibility for events or events outside of one's control.
4. **All-or-Nothing Thinking**: Thinking in black-and-white terms without taking into account the gray spaces in between.
5. **Mental Filtering**: Concentrating only on drawbacks while ignoring advantages.

These mental distortions contribute to a negative thought cycle that feeds worry and terror. By challenging and altering these incorrect thoughts, cognitive restructuring tries to end this vicious loop.

Cognitive restructuring steps:

1. **Recognize negative thoughts**: Understanding the negative ideas that fuel fear and anxiety is the first step in cognitive restructuring. Pay

attention to thinking patterns that come up frequently and record them in a journal.

2. **Examine Evidence**: Once negative ideas have been located, determine whether they are valid by going over the relevant data. Consider whether there is actual evidence supporting or refuting these ideas. People frequently come to discover that their fears are founded more on conjecture than reality.

3. **Challenge Negative Thoughts**: Reject negative thinking by posing challenging queries. Exists a different, more impartial viewpoint? What supporting data are there for this alternative viewpoint? Exist anymore reasons for the situation? This stage promotes a more realistic view and aids in dispelling erroneous notions.

4. **Replacing Negative Thoughts with Balanced and Rational Thoughts**: After confronting

negative thoughts, do the opposite. Look for proof to back up these fresh ideas and convictions. Recognizing advancements and successes is crucial, but excessive self-criticism must be avoided.

5. **Repetition and Practice**: Changing thought habits requires time and effort. Take part in everyday activities that require you to actively refute and combat negative beliefs. The new thought patterns will become stronger and more automatic with continued practice.

Strategies for Cognitive Restructuring:

1. **Cognitive journaling**: Keep a notebook to list negative ideas and their logical objections. To monitor progress and spot patterns, go back and review the entries frequently.
2. **Mindfulness Meditation**: Mindfulness aids in the development of uncritical awareness of thoughts. You can learn to recognize negative

thoughts as they come up and intentionally replace them with better, more logical thoughts with consistent practice.

3. **Role-playing**: Visualize yourself in frightening situations and practice responding and thinking logically. Role-playing enables you to create fresh thought processes and practice them in advance of situations in real life.

4. **Seeking Support**: Because cognitive restructuring can be difficult, it is advisable to get support from a counselor or therapist who specializes in cognitive-behavioral therapy (CBT). They can offer direction, criticism, and new methods to help the reorganization process.

Benefits of Cognitive Restructuring:

Beyond helping people overcome their fear and anxiety, cognitive restructuring has other advantages. It can raise self-esteem, strengthen problem-solving abilities, and advance psychological health in general. By altering thought patterns, people can adopt a more upbeat and adaptable mentality, which boosts resilience and enhances emotional control.

4.3 Meditation and Mindfulness: Cultivating Inner Strength

Developing inner strength has become more and more important for preserving a sense of balance, tranquility, and general well-being in today's fast-paced and demanding environment. People can develop this inner strength with the support of the effective tools and techniques that mindfulness and meditation provide. By incorporating these techniques into their daily lives, people can improve their capacity for dealing with difficulties, lessen stress, and discover more clarity and contentment. This article covers the ideas of mindfulness and meditation, stressing its advantages and offering helpful advice on how to incorporate it into daily life.

The act of paying attention to the current moment without passing judgment is known as mindfulness. It entails being completely conscious of one's ideas, emotions, physical sensations, and the environment. By practicing mindfulness, people can gain a better awareness of who they are and what has happened to them, which promotes self-compassion and resilience. Instead of reacting impulsively or becoming overwhelmed by stress, this technique enables people to respond to life's challenges with greater clarity and calm.

The formal practice of meditation, on the other hand, entails teaching the mind how to create a state of intense relaxation and concentrated attention. There are many different types of meditation, such as mindfulness, focused attention, and loving-kindness meditation. Although each method has particular advantages, they all aim to relax the mind and develop inner power. Regular meditation practice can increase emotional stability, create inner calm, and improve focus.

It's crucial to start a regular practice of mindfulness and meditation to start developing inner strength. Start by designating a definite time each day, even if it is only for a little while, for practicing. Locate a place that is peaceful and distraction-free where you can sit or lie down. Take a few deep breaths, close your eyes, and gradually focus on the present moment.

When practicing mindfulness meditation, keep an open mind and accept your thoughts and feelings as they come. Allow them to come and go as you bring your attention back to the breath or another focal area. The mind will occasionally stray, so once you become aware of it, gently bring it back to the present. This routine will help you become more adept at staying in the moment and detaching from unfavorable mental habits.

Along with formal meditation, practicing mindfulness in regular tasks has several advantages. While eating, pay close attention to the textures, flavors, and aromas of each bite. Participate fully in discussions while paying close attention to others. During walks or other physical exercises, pay attention to the sights, sounds, and textures of the surrounding area. You can create a stronger sense of gratitude, joy, and connection to the present now by incorporating mindfulness into these situations.

Beyond the brief periods of practice, mindfulness and meditation have many advantages. According to research, following these routines can lower stress levels, enhance emotional control, boost resilience, and improve general wellbeing. People who develop their inner fortitude are better able to deal with life's difficulties, which promotes inner fulfillment and inner tranquility.

Chapter 5
Overcoming Fear of Failure

A common and established emotion that frequently prevents people from reaching their full potential is the fear of failure. It can stop someone from acting, stop them from taking chances, and impede their own growth. It's important to realize that failure is a necessary component of life and that it may act as a powerful stimulant for development and achievement. By changing our point of view and implementing techniques to get over this fear, we may accept failure as a teaching opportunity and start a path toward self-improvement. This article examines many methods and attitudes that can be used to assist people in overcoming their fear of failing and realizing their full potential.

Understanding the Fear of Failure:

Our essential need for social acceptability, validation, and the need to avoid receiving negative feedback from others are the roots of the fear of failure. It frequently results from previous encounters or social forces that support the notion that failure is shameful or a sign of personal a lack of worth but it's important to understand that failure is a relative idea and doesn't decide how valuable we are as people. It is only a result that offers valuable lessons and chances for development.

Shifting Perspectives on Failure: In order to get over our fear of failing, we must change the way we think about what it means to fail. We might consider failure as a step on the path to success rather than seeing it as a personal setback. Every setback helps us get closer to our objectives by exposing what needs to be done better. We can regard failure as a learning opportunity that advances our professional and personal development by adopting a growth mindset.

Setting realistic goals:

Fear of failure frequently results from having unrealistic goals and worrying about what might happen if they are not met. We foster an environment that is conducive to growth by establishing goals that are achievable and achievable. We can gain momentum and improve our chances of success by breaking larger goals down into smaller, more doable activities. Celebrating minor successes along the way increases self-assurance and lessens the fear of failing.

Embracing Failure as a Learning Opportunity:

Failure should not be viewed as a measure of one's worth, but rather as an opportunity for vital learning. We can identify the contributing elements to our failures and take lessons from them by doing an objective analysis of them. We may make wise decisions and steer clear of the same risks in the future by thinking back on our errors and understanding the lessons they teach. Resilience and personal development are fostered by this iterative process.

Developing Resilience: Resilience is the capacity to overcome failures and challenges. It entails gaining emotional fortitude, adaptability, and optimism. Self-compassion, recognizing failure as a necessary part of life's path, and having a growth mindset are all necessary for building resilience. Exercise and mindfulness meditation are two examples of activities that can improve mental and emotional well-being and assist people overcome failure anxiety.

Taking Calculated Risks:

People frequently hesitate to take chances and take advantage of opportunities out of fear of failing. But success and growth frequently entail moving beyond of one's comfort zone. Making the distinction between measured risks and reckless behavior is crucial. We may make wise judgments and confidently move forward toward our objectives by performing in-depth study, making a strategy, and assessing the advantages and risks. By taking strategic chances, we can push our comfort zones and get over our failure phobia.

Building a Support Network:

We can considerably improve our capacity to get over the fear of failure by surrounding ourselves with a supporting network of family, friends, mentors, and like-minded people. Confidential people can offer us emotional support, a different perspective, and insightful information when we share our goals, worries, and disappointments with them. We can handle difficulties and be inspired to keep going by their support and helpful criticism.

5.1 Understanding the Fear of Failure: Its Impact on Success

A typical human emotion that can have a big impact on success is fear of failure. It is the trepidation and anxiety brought on by the potential for failing to achieve desired objectives or results. While fear is a natural emotion, allowing it to control one's thoughts and behavior can impede success and personal development.

The unwillingness to take chances is one of the main effects of failure fear. People who are terrified of failing frequently steer clear of opportunities or situations with unknown outcomes. This anxiety may result in a stale mindset that keeps people from considering novel ideas or pursuing challenging objectives. Success often requires moving beyond of one's comfort zone and accepting difficulties, but fear can operate as a roadblock, preventing advancement and success.

Lack of perseverance is another effect of fear of failure. People who are driven by fear may feel discouraged and give up easily when faced with setbacks or obstacles. Failures might be perceived by them as character faults or proof of incompetence, which would sap their motivation and confidence. In contrast, people who view failure as a teaching opportunity and an opportunity for personal development are more likely to persevere and succeed in the end.

In addition, a fear of failure may result in a poor perception of oneself. Worrying about failure all the time can damage self-esteem and lead to a self-fulfilling prophesy. People may inadvertently hinder their own efforts if they doubt their skills and expect to fail. People that adopt this negative perspective become too cautious and refrain from taking risks that could result in success, which can impede productivity, creativity, and innovation.

In addition, a person's willingness to take on new challenges and chances may be constrained by a fear of failure. People may develop an attitude of complacency and mediocrity as a result because they would rather remain in their comfort zones than face the chance of failing. As a result, they might pass up opportunities for advancement and fail to realize their full potential.

But it's crucial to understand that failure is a necessary component of learning and a stepping stone to achievement. Many successful people credit their successes to the lessons they gleaned from their disappointments in the past. People can conquer their fear and embrace risk-taking by reframing failure as a worthwhile experience and a chance for growth.

People can adopt a growth mindset to lessen the negative effects that failure fear has on their ability to succeed. This entails considering setbacks as transient learning experiences and chances to do better. By emphasizing progress rather than perfection, setting achievable goals and breaking them down into small steps might also assist people in getting over their fear. Getting help from mentors, coaches, or peers may be a great source of guidance and motivation.

5.2 Embracing Failure: A Catalyst for Growth and Learning

Although failure is frequently perceived as a bad and demoralizing experience, it may actually be a tremendous engine for learning and personal development. We open ourselves up to new opportunities and better achievements when we embrace failure and see it as a chance for growth. We may turn failures into steppingstones for success by changing the way we view failure.

Failure is necessary for growth in large part because it offers insightful criticism. When we fail, we learn what went wrong and can pinpoint areas that need improvement. With the help of this feedback, we may improve our tactics, sharpen our abilities, and gain a better understanding of our strengths and flaws. The light bulb's creator, Thomas Edison, once stated, "I have not failed. I recently discovered 10,000 methods that won't work. His viewpoint is a prime example of the mentality required to use failure as a launching pad for advancement.

Additionally, failure develops fortitude and character. It teaches us to endure through hardship and overcome obstacles. We gain tenacity and determination when we encounter failure and don't give up. In the long run, having these traits can help you succeed more in any effort. From business owners to athletes, many successful people had many setbacks before succeeding. Every setback served as a teaching opportunity that brought them one step closer to their intended results.

Failure also forces us to step outside of our comfort zones. Failure becomes a natural part of the process when we take risks and venture into the unknown. It motivates us to push limits, think creatively, and explore new ideas. By accepting failure, we develop a growth mentality that encourages creativity and ongoing learning. This way of thinking helps us take advantage of opportunities and adjust to changing circumstances.

Nevertheless, accepting failure does not entail actively seeking it out or reveling in mediocrity. It entails realizing that failure is a necessary component of the road to success. It calls for a change in mindset where failures are viewed as important experiences rather than as flaws in oneself. Accepting failure also entails accepting accountability for our actions, learning from our errors, and making the required improvements.

5.3 Building Resilience: Bouncing Back from Setbacks

There are plenty of challenges to overcome in life, and failures are an unavoidable part of the path. Learning to rebound from setbacks is an essential ability for developing resilience, regardless of whether it's a personal failure, a career setback, or a challenging life event. Resilience, which is the capacity to overcome obstacles and bounce back, is crucial to our success and general well-being. We can confront obstacles head-on, take their lessons to heart, and ultimately become stronger through cultivating resilience.

Creating a positive mentality is a crucial component in developing resilience. Try to keep your attention on the chances for improvement and learning rather than lingering on the negative aspects of a setback. You can regard setbacks as transitory difficulties rather than insurmountable hurdles by adopting an optimistic mindset. Keep in mind that setbacks are merely a part of the path to success; they are not a reflection of your value or skill.

Building a solid support network is a crucial component of resilience. When facing challenges, surrounding yourself with supportive friends and family can make all the difference. Consult with your friends, family, and/or mentors for help, insight, and support. Their experience and empathy can open your eyes to new ideas and provide you the emotional support you require while facing difficult situations.

When developing resilience, self-care is equally crucial. It's important to take care of your physical and mental health because setbacks can be emotionally draining. Whether it's exercising, meditating, spending time in nature, or engaging in hobbies, do what makes you happy. You may recharge and face setbacks with a clearer, more focused mind by taking care of yourself.

Resilience and adaptation go hand in hand. You can overcome failures with greater ease if you are flexible and open to change. Be open to investigating various strategies and viewpoints as opposed to being fixated on one particular option. Even in the face of difficulty, this flexibility can help you come up with creative ideas and adjust to new situations.

Developing problem-solving abilities is an essential part of increasing resilience. Consider setbacks as chances for learning and growth rather than as obstacles. Create a list of possible solutions after doing a thorough examination of the problem. Take action by breaking the issue down into doable steps. Every small step you take will increase your self-assurance and resiliency, making you a stronger and more resilient version of yourself in the end.

Gratitude exercises can also help people become more resilient. Even when things go wrong, there are frequently positive things to be thankful for. Developing a thankfulness mentality might help you change your perspective from what went wrong in your life to what is going great in it. You can keep a sense of perspective and hope through trying times by focusing on the positives.

Finally, it's crucial to keep in mind that developing resilience is a journey rather than a final goal. Life will inevitably be filled with setbacks, but you can build the resilience necessary to overcome them by viewing them as chances for personal development and learning. Every obstacle you overcome strengthens your resilience muscles and gives you the necessary tools to tackle new problems with assurance.

Chapter 6

Navigating Social Anxiety

Social anxiety is a common condition that affects millions of people worldwide. It is characterized by an intense opposition to social situations and a persistent concern with rejection or public humiliation. It can be difficult to deal with social anxiety, but with the correct tools and support, individuals can learn to control their anxiety and have happy, meaningful lives.

Learning more about social anxiety is one of the first stages in dealing with it. Individuals can identify their triggers and create coping methods by becoming aware of the signs and causes of social anxiety. It's important to keep in mind that social anxiety is a treatable mental health problem rather than a character flaw or weakness.

Creating a support network is essential for coping with social anxiety. People can share their experiences and learn from others in a safe and understanding environment provided by friends, family, or support groups. Making connections with others who experience comparable difficulties can help reduce feelings of isolation and offer insightful advice on how to control anxiety.

Another essential component in overcoming social anxiety is therapy. A strategy that is frequently used, cognitive-behavioral therapy (CBT), concentrates on recognizing and altering negative thought patterns and behaviors. In a safe and encouraging setting, people can learn to challenge their anxious ideas, practice relaxation techniques, and gradually face their fears through counseling.

To effectively manage social anxiety, one must practice self-care. Exercise, meditation, or socializing are examples of activities that might help relieve stress and enhance general mental health. Making self-care a top concern enables people to recharge and develop resilience, which is crucial when dealing with social situations that could cause anxiety.

Gradual exposure is a useful method for controlling social anxiety. This entails introducing oneself to dreaded social situations gradually and methodically. Individuals can gradually raise their amount of exposure while starting with small, manageable measures to help them gain confidence and lessen their fear.

It's crucial to fight self-defeating thoughts and practice self-compassion. People who struggle with social anxiety frequently have an unreasonably high standard for themselves and worry all the time that they will mess up or offend someone. Anxiety can be reduced and a more positive sense of oneself is possible by learning to reframe difficult ideas and treat oneself with kindness and understanding.

The key to overcoming social anxiety is to become an effective communicator. People might feel more empowered and experience less anxiety in social situations by learning to state their demands and boundaries in an assertive manner. Building relationships and lowering self-consciousness can also be achieved through the practice of attentive listening and meaningful discussion.

To treat social anxiety, medication can be recommended. Medication for depression or anxiety can help with symptoms and make it easier to interact with people in social circumstances. Working closely with a healthcare practitioner is essential to determining the best drug and dosage for each patient.

Finally, it's important to practice self-kindness and patience while you manage social anxiety. It takes time and work to overcome anxiety, and failures are frequent. In order to stay motivated and promote a good outlook, it might be helpful to recognize and rejoice in tiny triumphs and progress, no matter how small.

6.1 Social Anxiety: The Fear of Judgment and Rejection

A mental illness referred to as social anxiety is defined by an overwhelming fear of being criticized, judged, or rejected in social settings. It affects a person's everyday life and well-being significantly and goes beyond simple shyness or introversion. Social situations frequently cause anguish and discomfort for those with social anxiety, which results in avoidance behaviors and a lower quality of life.

At its root, social anxiety is a dread of criticism and rejection. People who experience this syndrome are continuously concerned about how other people view them and worry that they will be judged, laughed at, or otherwise degraded. Parties, public speaking engagements, job interviews, or even simple chats with strangers can all cause this fear to surface. Individuals with social anxiety go to great lengths to avoid these situations because they are so afraid of being negatively evaluated.

Social anxiety can have significant effects on a person's life. Avoiding social engagements may harm relationships, both personal and professional. Due to the anxiety of being rejected or falling short of social expectations, it can become challenging to establish new connections or maintain existing ones. This can exacerbate anxiety by causing feelings of loneliness and isolation.

Social anxiety can have many and varied causes. It might have its roots in adverse childhood experiences like being bullied or receiving severe criticism, which build a strong dread of being judged and rejected.

Embarrassing or traumatic experiences can also play a role in the development of social anxiety. Additionally, some personality qualities, such a drive toward perfectionism or a low sense of self-worth, can increase a person's risk of developing social anxiety.

When treating social anxiety, cognitive behavioral therapy (CBT) is frequently used as the main method. CBT enables people to question and alter unfavorable thought patterns and beliefs that fuel their anxiety. Through exposure therapy, people can progressively confront their fears in a safe and encouraging setting, which enables them to gradually improve their coping skills and lessen their anxiety.

Medication might be recommended to treat the symptoms of social anxiety in addition to treatment. Selective serotonin reuptake inhibitors (SSRIs), a type of antidepressant, are commonly used to reduce anxiety and improve overall well-being. To decide on the best course of therapy, a trained healthcare expert should always be consulted before taking any drug.

In addition to therapy and medication, people with social anxiety can use a variety of self-help techniques. To address anxiety symptoms right away, these include using relaxation techniques like deep breathing and mindfulness. Regular physical activity has also been demonstrated to lower anxiety and enhance general mental health. Getting support from friends, family, or support groups can provide you access to a useful network of sympathetic people who can encourage and direct you.

It is crucial to realize that social anxiety is a mental health condition that calls for understanding and support. It may be difficult for people who have never personally dealt with social anxiety to understand the suffering it causes. We can create an atmosphere where people with social anxiety feel understood and accepted by encouraging a caring and inclusive society, giving them the confidence, they need to face their concerns and lead fulfilling lives.

6.2 Building Social Confidence: Tips and Techniques

Our personal and professional life both depend on social confidence. It gives us the ability to engage with others, form deep connections, and seize opportunities. However, a lot of individuals suffer from social anxiety and find it difficult to get past their fears. Fortunately, there are a number of useful advice and methods that can support social confidence development. You may progressively raise your level of comfort in social situations and grow more confident by adopting these activities into your daily life.

1. **Self-Awareness**: To begin, work on developing self-awareness. Recognize your socially secure and less confident regions as well as your strengths and flaws. Determine the particular triggers that make you uncomfortable or anxious, and accept them without passing judgment. You will be better able to confront and overcome your worries as a result of this insight.

2. **Set Realistic Goals**: Establish modest, doable objectives that progressively take you outside of your comfort zone. Start by striking up conversations with friends or getting involved in social events that you find interesting, for instance. Your confidence will inevitably increase as you reach these objectives, motivating you to take on bigger challenges.

3. **Practice Active Listening**: By working on active listening, you can improve your communication abilities. Maintain eye contact, listen intently, and show real interest in what people are saying. Positive social relationships are promoted through active listening, which not only deepens your comprehension of others but also makes them feel valued and respected.

4. **Positive Self-Talk**: Pay attention to the thoughts that run through your head and swap out the negative ones for positive ones. Recall your qualities, successes, and effective social interactions from the past. This

mental change will gradually increase your confidence and lessen self-doubt.

5. **Body Language**: Communication is greatly influenced by nonverbal cues. Maintain a calm, open, and genuine grin while making eye contact. Positive body language not only conveys confidence to others but also helps you seem more approachable.

6. **Seek Support**: Don't be afraid to ask friends, family, or a therapist for support. With someone you can trust, express your worries and concerns and ask for their advice. A different viewpoint might occasionally offer useful advice and inspiration for overcoming social anxiety.

7. **Gradual Exposure**: Introduce anxious situations to oneself gradually. Start with low-pressure social gatherings and eventually advance to more difficult ones. Your confidence in your social skills will grow with each positive experience, enabling you to take on bigger challenges in society.

8. **Embrace Mistakes**: Understand that making mistakes is a necessary element of learning. Don't let them make you feel less confident; instead, embrace them as chances for improvement. Recognize that social errors are commonplace and don't reflect poorly on you as a person.

9. **Look after Yourself**: Give self-care activities a high priority if they will improve your general wellbeing. Get regular exercise, sufficient rest, a healthy diet, and relaxation techniques like deep breathing or meditation. Your social confidence increases naturally when you're intellectually and physically healthy.

10. **Celebrate improvement**: Regardless of how small your improvement may be, acknowledge it and celebrate it. Give yourself praise for each action you complete to increase your social comfort. Think back on your accomplishments and remind yourself of the progress you've made in a favorable direction.

Keep in mind that gaining social confidence is a long process that calls for endurance and patience. Accept the adventure, show yourself empathy, and keep pushing your limits. You'll gain the desired level of social confidence with time and effort, which will help you access exciting and worthwhile social situations.

6.3 Expanding Social Networks: Overcoming Isolation

Increasing social networks has become crucial for fighting isolation in the current digital era. A strong network of relationships is essential to our general wellbeing and mental health because humans are fundamentally social organisms. But isolation can be a problem, especially in modern times where people may feel cut off even if they are continuously surrounded by others. Thankfully, there are many strategies for overcoming this feeling of seclusion and growing our social networks.

The emergence of social media platforms is one of the biggest factors in the growth of social networks. Through websites like

Facebook, Twitter, and Instagram, people may communicate with friends, family, and even complete strangers from around the globe. People can converse, exchange experiences, and establish new connections via these platforms. Through social media, users can also join online communities or groups with similar interests, pastimes, or concerns. This gives like-minded people a way to connect and support one another.

By taking part in regional community events, social networks can be expanded in another efficient method. Many different events, festivals, and chances to volunteer are organized by communities so that individuals may get together, meet new people, and have meaningful connections. People can interact with their neighbors, create a sense of belonging, and overcome loneliness by actively taking part in these events.

Getting involved in clubs, organizations, or hobby groups is yet another fantastic way to broaden social networks. These organizations, whether they are sports teams, literature clubs, or photography groups, give people a chance to connect with others who share their hobbies and interests. Opportunities for bonding and establishing enduring friendships are created by frequent gatherings and shared activities.

Finding support groups can also be incredibly helpful for overcoming isolation. People who are dealing with the same difficulties, such as sorrow, mental health problems, or chronic illnesses, can get together in support groups. These groups offer a secure setting where people may open up about their experiences, find comfort, and create a network of similar individuals.

Finally, volunteering or participating in charitable endeavors is a great way to meet new people while also giving back to the community. Volunteering for a cause that shares one's ideals enables people to meet others who share their values and work together to achieve a common objective, establishing a feeling of community and extending social networks.

Chapter 7

Overcoming Fear of Change

Change is an inevitable part of life. From personal growth to technological advancements, change surrounds us constantly but a lot of people realize that the fear of change paralyzes them. People may hesitate to pursue new possibilities and experiences because of their overwhelming fear of the future and the uncertainty that comes with change. However, mastering this fear is crucial for both success and personal development.

Rethinking our perspective is a powerful way to get over our fear of change. We ought to see change as an opportunity for progress and self-improvement rather than as a threat. Accepting change enables us to broaden our perspectives, acquire new abilities, and unlock our hidden potential. We might learn to see change as an exciting adventure rather than something to be afraid by changing our perspective.

Another strategy is to divide the change into smaller parts. It can be difficult to keep the entire process in mind when dealing with a big change. By breaking things down into manageable pieces, we may take on each one individually, generating momentum and self-assurance as we go. We strengthen our ability to successfully handle change by acknowledging each modest win.

When conquering the fear of change, it is equally essential to look for support from others. Having a strong network of family, friends, or mentors at our sides can give us comfort and encouragement when things go tough. Sharing our fears and uncertainties with reliable people can help us achieve clarity and confidence by offering insightful suggestions, pointers, and viewpoints.

Additionally, it's critical to keep in mind that failure is a necessary component of the transition process. The fear of change can be reduced by acknowledging that setbacks and difficulties are common. We become more resilient and willing to take risks when we see failure as an opportunity to learn and advance. Each setback advances us toward success and gets us one step closer to our objectives.

The final step in conquering the fear of change is self-care. Stress and anxiety can be lessened by partaking in relaxing activities like meditation, exercise, or hobbies. Taking care of our physical and mental health improves our capacity for good adaptation and change management.

7.1 Fear of the Unknown: Embracing Life Transitions

Unknown-related fear is a natural human reaction that is established in our psyche. The fear is frequently brought on by changes in our lives, no matter how big or small, as we deal with unfamiliar terrain and unexpected results. However, accepting these changes might spur on personal development and change.

It takes bravery and the ability to let go of the known to step into the unknown. We have the chance to redefine ourselves and find novel abilities during these times of transformation. We may broaden our horizons, build resiliency, and foster adaptation by accepting change.

Starting a new job, relocating to a new place, or even ending a relationship are all examples of transitions. Every change has its own set of chances and difficulties. We may go from a fear-based perspective to one that is curious and exciting by changing the way we see things.

Although uncertainty might be unsettling, it is frequently a sign of development and advancement. By taking a chance on the unknown, we expose ourselves to opportunities we never would have considered. We learn to trust ourselves and gain a better awareness of our capabilities by accepting life's adjustments.

7.2 Embracing Change: Strategies for Adaptability

In the continuously changing world of today, acceptance of change is crucial. It requires that people and organizations create adaptive techniques that will enable them to flourish in the face of uncertainty. Fostering a growth attitude is one important tactic. This way of thinking helps people to see difficulties as opportunities for learning and development. People can stay flexible and adaptive by viewing change as an opportunity to gain new knowledge and abilities.

Building an innovative culture is a further beneficial tactic. People can adjust to new circumstances more quickly when an organization fosters creativity and experimentation. Innovative ideas and solutions can be produced by embracing other viewpoints and encouraging collaboration.

Additionally, it's important to keep up with new trends and knowledge. Understanding how technology and industries are changing enables people and organizations to anticipate and adapt to changing demands. The building of a strong foundation for flexibility can be facilitated through networking with professionals in adjacent industries, participating in workshops, and continuing education.

Additionally, it's important to build resilience. Change frequently entails difficulties and difficulties. Resilient people recover from hardships, learning from mistakes and disappointments, and using them as stepping stones on the path to achievement. People can negotiate change with resilience and calm by developing emotional intelligence and stress management skills.

7.3 Thriving in Uncertainty: Seizing Change's Opportunities

Uncertainty has become a frequent companion in today's quick-paced and ever-changing environment. Success now depends on one's ability to deal with change, whether it comes from pandemics, global economic shifts, or technology developments. Rather than fearing uncertainty, forward-thinking individuals and organizations have learned to embrace it as a catalyst for growth and innovation.

The development of an adaptable mindset is a crucial component of thriving in uncertainty. We can find opportunities that may not have been there before by being open to new possibilities rather than holding fast to fixed plans or rejecting change. Flexibility and a willingness to leave our comfort zones are necessary for change adaptation, which can result in both personal and professional growth.

In addition, accepting uncertainty motivates us to take a proactive rather than a reactive approach. We may position ourselves to take advantage of opportunities that occur from unanticipated events by predicting and planning for such interruptions. Continuously scanning the surroundings, keeping an eye on trends, and keeping up with new technology or market movements are all part of this proactive strategy.

Additionally important to prospering in an unpredictable world are networking and collaboration. Making connections with varied people and working together can promote creativity and lead to original ideas. We can better adapt to change and find new opportunities for progress by leveraging the pooled intelligence and viewpoints of others.

Chapter 8

Managing Fear in Relationships

For you to keep up a happy and meaningful relationship with your partner, managing your fear in relationships is important. Fear frequently results from a lack of trust, unpleasant events in the past, or self-insecurities. Open dialogue is essential for addressing and overcoming these fears. By discussing your concerns and fears with your partner, you open the door to support and understanding.

Developing trust is essential for overcoming fear. Encourage transparency and openness in your interactions so that a strong foundation of trust can grow. It's also important to identify and deal with any underlying insecurities that might be causing dread. Understanding and conquering these fears can be helped by self-reflection and personal growth.

Self-care and taking care of your own wellbeing can also aid in managing fear. Take part in enjoyable activities, keep a solid support structure in place, and learn self-compassion. This helps you develop a sense of security and self-assurance, which loosens the relationship's grasp on fear.

It's important to remember that fear is a normal human feeling and that you should respect and affirm your partner's fears as well. Make an environment where both parties feel comfortable talking about their issues and cooperating to find solutions.

Managing fear in relationships becomes a continuous process of understanding and growth by fostering trust, promoting open communication, addressing fears, and engaging in self-care. In the end, it may result in a stronger bond and a union based on love, trust, and assistance to one another.

8.1 Fear of Intimacy: Overcoming Emotional Barriers

A typical emotional hurdle that may hinder deep connections and relationships is a fear of intimacy. It is caused by a number of things, including past traumas, rejection fear, and low self-esteem. It takes reflection and a gradual shift toward vulnerability to get over this sense of fear. Finding the source of the fear's origins and overcoming them with the aid of a therapist or support group is one strategy. Building self-worth and self-confidence is essential because it enables people to believe they are worthy of affection and connection. Establishing trust and intimacy also requires learning effective communication skills and establishing clear boundaries. The fear of intimacy can be overcome by taking modest risks, opening up gradually, and allowing oneself to be seen as one truly is. It's crucial to keep in mind that closeness develops gradually and that patience and self-compassion are essential. People can have more meaningful connections and relationships by addressing the underlying emotional hurdles.

8.2 Communication and Vulnerability: Building Trust

Building trust is based on effective communication, and being vulnerable is essential to this process. People can engage in a safe area where they can be open and honest about their feelings, anxieties and challenges. People show their trust in others by being vulnerable, which encourages closer relationships and fosters empathy.

By lowering misunderstandings and tearing down barriers, vulnerability improves communication. Individuals are able to openly express their wants, expectations, and boundaries, which promotes respect and understanding between others. Additionally, when leaders show vulnerability, they set a good example for their employees and promote candid communication and teamwork.

Communication requires both attentive listening and empathic replies in order to develop trust. People are more likely to reciprocate by expressing their vulnerabilities when they feel truly heard and understood. People feel supported and valued as a result of this interchange, which cultivates a trusting environment.

It's crucial to keep in mind that fragility calls for kindness and discretion. Building trust by upholding confidentiality and respecting boundaries promotes ongoing openness. In the end, trust can only be fostered via good communication and vulnerability, which also nurtures relationships and promotes both personal and professional development.

8.3 Healing Past Wounds: Letting Go of Fear in Relationships

Our prior relationships can leave us with significant scars that frequently endure, influencing how we interact with people now and in the future. Genuine connection and intimacy might be hampered by these wounds, which are fed by fear. But maintaining healthy relationships and finding fulfillment depend on mending old hurts.

It's vital to recognize and comprehend the causes of our worries in order to start the healing process. It may be challenging to fully open up to others due to past traumas or unpleasant experiences that have left you feeling vulnerable and distrustful. We can progressively release the underlying fears and feelings associated with these wounds by investigating them with empathy and self-compassion.

A key component of recovery is forgiveness. It entails letting go of animosity and the suffering brought on by the past's wrongs. Even if it doesn't justify other people's behavior, forgiveness frees us from the weight of resentment and enables us to go on. It is a potent self-care practice that enables us to regain our power and make room for fresh, better connections.

Another crucial phase is to develop self-worth and self-love. When we value and cherish who we are, we establish boundaries to protect us from additional hurt. Having a strong sense of self-worth enables us to select partners who share our beliefs and treat us with respect. Additionally, it enables us to negotiate relationships with greater awareness and discernment and to see warning signs.

In order to promote relationship healing and connection, communication is essential. We foster empathy and understanding by being upfront and honest about our needs, fears, and desires. Active listening is a crucial component of effective communication because it enables our partners to express their own feelings and experiences. This shared vulnerability can strengthen the bond between the two people and create a secure and encouraging environment for them both.

Along the way to healing, self-compassion and patience are crucial. It requires time and effort to mend old wounds. It demands that we be kind to ourselves and accept the possibility of incremental improvement. Having a network of friends, family, or even professionals at our sides can offer the direction and inspiration need to travel the path of healing.

Chapter 9

Cultivating Courage and Self-Confidence

People who possess courage and confidence are better equipped to face problems in life and persevere in their pursuit of their goals. These attributes can only be developed by reflection, practice, and a dedication to personal development. People can overcome challenges, face fears, and seize chances that result in success on the personal and professional levels by strengthening their courage and confidence.

It is essential to accept and face fears in order to develop courage and self-confidence. Fear frequently serves as a roadblock, preventing people from taking chances or moving outside of their comfort zones. However, people might begin to undermine the strength of these concerns by identifying them and comprehending where they came from. By gradually confronting concerns, whether by baby steps or calculated risks, one can increase comfort zones and develop courage.

The development of self-confidence also involves being aware of and grateful for one's abilities and achievements. Celebrating individual accomplishments, no matter how minor, supports a healthy self-image. It is crucial to keep in mind that everyone has special talents and skills, and that by accepting them, people can develop a sense of self-worth and self-assurance in their abilities.

Another useful technique for developing courage and confidence is to challenge oneself and set realistic goals. People can build resilience and unlock potential by pushing boundaries and taking on new challenges. No matter how big or small, each success adds to confidence and fosters the idea that one can overcome obstacles in the future.

Having a strong support system of friends, mentors, and role models is also essential for developing courage and self-assurance. Relationships that are supportive and encouraging offer a nurturing environment where people can discover their strengths and get advice and support. Learning from the experiences of those who have faced challenges and succeeded can encourage and inspire people on their own journey.

An often-overlooked component of developing bravery and self-confidence is practicing self-care and self-compassion. Maintaining a good mindset and a resilient attitude requires taking care of one's physical, mental, and emotional well-being. A healthy self-image and more confidence can be attained through engaging in enjoyable and relaxing activities, practicing mindfulness, and adopting self-compassion while facing failure or setbacks.

Finally, developing courage and confidence calls for persistence and a growth attitude. It is essential to view obstacles and failures as chances for development. Failure comes naturally on the path to success, and by viewing setbacks as stepping stones, people can build resilience and the drive to keep going.

9.1 Developing Inner Strength: The Power of Courage

When faced with difficulties in life, people can draw on their inner strength and get beyond problems thanks to the force of courage. Fear is a natural emotion, but courage is the capacity to face it head-on and overcome it. It is a quality that encourages people to forge ahead, take chances, and confront difficulty head-on.

There are courageous people around, and it's not just in acts of bravery. To stand up for what one believes in, to speak out against injustice, or to pursue one's aspirations despite uncertainty and misgivings needs bravery. It takes vulnerability and the determination to move beyond of one's comfort zone to cultivate inner strength through courage.

Understanding and accepting fear is a vital part of developing courage. People are able to investigate the underlying causes of their concerns and take steps to overcome them once they have acknowledged them. People might progressively gain resilience and the inner fortitude required to overcome life's obstacles by facing their fears.

The development of courage also requires a strong sense of self-worth and self-compassion. Having confidence in oneself and one's ability paves the way for taking chances and accepting new experiences. Contrarily, self-compassion enables people to be kind to and understanding of themselves, even in the face of failures or losses. It motivates people to keep going forward and to learn from their failures.

Having a strong support system around you are another essential aspect of gaining courage and inner strength. Having a solid support network offers inspiration, direction, and certainty during trying times. Sharing fears and weaknesses with dependable people can lighten the load and give you a new outlook on overcoming challenges.

It's crucial to keep in mind that growing courageously as an inner strength is a constant process. It demands persistence and practice. Personal development and resilience are enhanced by every step taken in the direction of overcoming anxieties and accepting challenges. As people develop bravery, they unlock their potential and come to understand that they are capable of accomplishing amazing things.

9.2 Techniques and Practices for Increasing Self-Confidence

Increasing self-confidence is a worthwhile endeavor that can have a good effect on many areas of our lives. People can cultivate and improve their confidence by using specific methods and activities. The power of encouraging yourself is one technique. People can intentionally rewire their mindset to be more self-assured by consciously substituting positive affirmations and statements for negative ideas and beliefs.

The act of setting and attaining modest, doable goals is also beneficial. Reaching these objectives gives one a sense of success and increases self-confidence. Additionally, taking on new challenges and pushing beyond of one's comfort zone promotes personal development and a stronger self-belief.

Building self-confidence depends heavily on practicing self-care. Exercise, meditation, and leisure pursuits are a few examples of things that might help you feel better about yourself and boost your self-esteem. Having a friendly and motivating environment around you might also help you feel more confident.

Learning from mistakes and past experiences can also be transformational. Resilience and self-assurance can be developed by accepting setbacks as opportunities for progress and realizing that everyone suffers difficulties.

Self-compassion training is equally crucial. In contrast to self-criticism, treating oneself with compassion and understanding encourages perseverance in the face of challenges.

Finally, getting expert assistance, such as counseling or coaching, can offer invaluable direction and support on the path to boosting self-confidence. These experts can offer specialized methods and techniques based on specific client requirements.

9.3 Taking Action: Stepping Outside the Comfort Zone

A crucial component of self-development is acting and moving beyond of one's comfort zone. Stepping outside one's comfort zone allows people to broaden their horizons, develop resilience, and realize their actual potential, but it takes pushing limits, accepting difficulties, and venturing into uncharted territory.

One can get new abilities, information, and experiences through exploring unexplored area. It offers a chance to pick up new skills and adjust to challenging circumstances, encouraging creativity and innovation. Experimenting outside of one's comfort zone increases self-assurance and self-belief as people succeed in new endeavors and conquer challenges.

Additionally, stepping outside of one's comfort zone might result in personal growth. It relieves the monotony of routine and inspires people to welcome change and adapt to novel surroundings. It promotes a growth mentality and supports lifelong learning.

It can be difficult to leave your comfort zone, though. People are frequently held back by fear, self-doubt, and uncertainty. These obstacles must be overcome with bravery, tenacity, and a willingness to take chances. It entails making plans, creating objectives, and moving deliberately in the direction of personal development.

Chapter 10

Sustaining Progress and Embracing a Fearless Life

Maintaining development and living a brave life are two related ideas that enable people to fulfill their potential and lead satisfying lives. Maintaining momentum and constant improvement in a variety of facets of life, such as interpersonal connections, career advancement, and personal growth, is necessary for sustained progress.

A growth mindset that views obstacles as chances for growth and learning is necessary for sustained advancement. It necessitates having specific objectives, making workable strategies, and persevering through challenges and disappointments. People can successfully traverse the inevitable ups and downs of life by developing a resilient attitude and asking for help when necessary.

Stepping outside of one's comfort zone and embracing new experiences with courage and tenacity are essential to leading a fearless life. It entails letting go of limiting preconceptions about oneself and accepting uncertainty. People can access a world of opportunities and personal development by facing their fears and taking measured risks.

Living fearlessly doesn't mean acting reckless; rather, it entails making thoughtful choices and having confidence in one's capacity to overcome obstacles. People can step outside of their comfort zones, become more resilient, and have more faith in their capacity to handle whatever comes their way by tackling their fears head-on.

Maintaining progress and living a fearless life go hand in hand since making progress frequently calls for taking risks and embracing uncertainty. People who have a courageous perspective can maintain development by always looking for possibilities for improvement, adjusting to change, and accepting new challenges. A fearless existence then feeds back into sustained progress as successes and personal development give one the assurance and drive to keep living fearlessly.

10.1 Maintaining Fearlessness: Strategies for Long-Term Success

Long-term success depends on maintaining a fearless attitude since it enables people to overcome challenges and seize opportunities. The development of a growth mindset is one tactic. Accepting the idea that skills can be improved through commitment and effort enables people to face obstacles head-on without giving in to fear. Furthermore, having specific objectives and a plan for achieving them gives one a sense of purpose and direction, which encourages fearlessness. It is essential to surround oneself with a community of like-minded people who inspire and promote personal development. Individuals can benefit from the wisdom and experiences of their collective relationships by cultivating them. Another successful tactic is routinely stepping beyond of one's comfort zone. One's capabilities are increased and resilience is built through taking calculated risks and facing concerns. Identification and management of fears are aided by mindfulness and self-reflection practices.

People can create efficient coping systems by comprehending the underlying reasons of fear. Last but not least, by refocusing attention from perfection to progress, accepting failure as a learning opportunity rather than a setback fosters bravery. These techniques can help people overcome their fears and pave the road for long-term success.

10.2 Embracing Growth: Continuing the Journey Beyond Fears

Embracing growth is a transformative journey that takes us beyond our fears and propels us towards personal and professional development. It calls for us to leave our comfort zones and approach the uncharted with curiosity and openness. By doing this, we broaden our perspectives, unearth fresh opportunities, and realize our full potential.

Fear is one of the largest barriers to accepting growth. We can be discouraged from taking chances and pursuing our aspirations by our fears of failure, rejection, and the unknown. Recognizing that growth frequently lies on the other side of fear is crucial, though. Faced with our concerns, we challenge ourselves to go beyond our comfort zones and learn what we are truly capable of.

The path to accepting growth is not always simple. Resilience and a readiness to take lessons from both successes and setbacks are necessary. Positive or negative, every experience teaches us important lessons that advance our personal and professional development. We can turn failures into stepping stones on the path to success by changing our perspective and seeing obstacles as chances for progress.

Additionally, embracing progress entails seeking out novel encounters and consistently enhancing our knowledge and abilities. It necessitates a dedication to personal growth as well as a lifelong learning mentality. This could entail taking classes, going to workshops, looking for a mentor, or doing some introspection. We can adapt to the constantly shifting environment around us and stay one step ahead of the curve by continually investing in ourselves.

Additionally, in order to embrace growth, we must surround ourselves with a network of people who will encourage and challenge us. We may create an atmosphere that promotes growth and inspires us to achieve new heights by seeking out mentors and like-minded people who share our beliefs and objectives.

10.3 Inspiring Others: Spreading Courage and Empowerment

The ability to inspire others is a talent with unimaginable potential in a world full of obstacles and uncertainties. When we inspire people with courage and confidence, we kindle a spark that enables them to find their inner strength and face their fears. Each of us has the power to have a great effect on others around us, inspiring them to aim high and have faith in their own skills.

Setting a positive example for others is one of the most effective methods to motivate others. We become a source of inspiration for those who may be experiencing difficulty when we show courage and perseverance in the face of difficulty. By telling others about how we overcame difficulties, we offer a path for them to follow and inspire them to believe that they, too, are capable of overcoming any difficulty.

Another essential component of inspiring people is empowerment. People that are empowered have the self-assurance and believe in themselves to achieve their dreams. Encouragement, attentive listening to their thoughts, and offering assistance when required might accomplish this. When we give others the power, we start a chain reaction that extends well beyond our own sphere of influence and motivates others to do the same for others in their near area.

When used properly, words can have great power. We may foster a healthy environment that promotes resilience and personal growth by using our words to inspire and uplift those around us. Simple deeds of kindness, like speaking encouraging words or praising someone's achievements, can have a profound impact on someone's life. A heartfelt compliment or a sincere declaration of confidence in someone's skills has the capacity to motivate them to go beyond their perceived limits and pursue greatness.

Inspiring locations can also be discovered. The world is full with inspiration waiting to be found, whether it be in the form of literature, music, art, or nature. Sharing our own sources of inspiration with others can open their eyes to new ideas and rekindle their love for living. We foster an environment where everyone's distinctive abilities and talents may flourish by accepting diversity and appreciating individuality, motivating others to follow suit.

It's critical to keep in mind that finding inspiration is a never-ending adventure. As we motivate others, their development and tenacity motivate us as well. It is a reciprocal process that spreads like wildfire and feeds off good energy. We can start a chain reaction of inspiration that can change people's lives and improve the world

if we consistently look for ways to inspire
and empower others around us.